KENTUCKY

HELLO U.S.A.

by Dottie Brown

 Lerner Publications Company

You'll find this picture of a tulip tree flower at the beginning of each chapter in this book. The tulip tree got its name from its flowers, which look like tulips. Wood from this tall tree is very valuable. The tulip tree replaced the Kentucky coffee tree as Kentucky's state tree in 1994.

Cover (left): The Kentucky Derby at Churchill Downs, Louisville. Cover (right): My Old Kentucky Home—said to be the inspiration for the Kentucky state song—in Bardstown. Pages 2–3: Downtown Louisville. Page 3: Cumberland Falls State Park.

This book is available in two editions:
Library binding by Lerner Publications Company, a division of Lerner Publishing Group
Soft cover by First Avenue Editions, an imprint of Lerner Publishing Group
241 First Avenue North
Minneapolis, MN 55401 U.S.A.

Website address: www.lernerbooks.com

Library of Congress Cataloging-in-Publication Data

Brown, Dottie, 1957–
    Kentucky / by Dottie Brown. (Rev. and expanded 2nd ed.)
       p.   cm. — (Hello U.S.A.)
    Includes index.
    Summary: An introduction to the land, history, people, economy, and environment of Kentucky.
       ISBN: 0–8225–4083–5 (lib. bdg. : alk. paper)
       ISBN: 0–8225–0781–1 (pbk. : alk. paper)
       1. Kentucky—Juvenile literature. [1. Kentucky.] I. Title. II. Series.
    F451.3 .B76 2002
    976.9—dc21   2001006021

Manufactured in the United States of America
1 2 3 4 5 6 – JR – 07 06 05 04 03 02

CONTENTS

THE LAND

The Bluegrass State

"Elbow room!" cried Daniel Boone, Kentucky's famous frontiersman. He had heard many stories about the wilderness that the Cherokee Indians called *Kentahteh*, meaning "land of tomorrow." Boone longed to settle in a place with open land and lots of game—and without lots of people. So he took a hunting trip to the area that later became Kentucky and decided to make it his home.

Kentucky is nicknamed the Bluegrass State after a grass that grows in its Bluegrass Region. The grass isn't really blue, but in the spring it grows tiny blue buds. Fields of bluegrass *(opposite page)* and farms *(right)* fill Kentucky's open spaces.

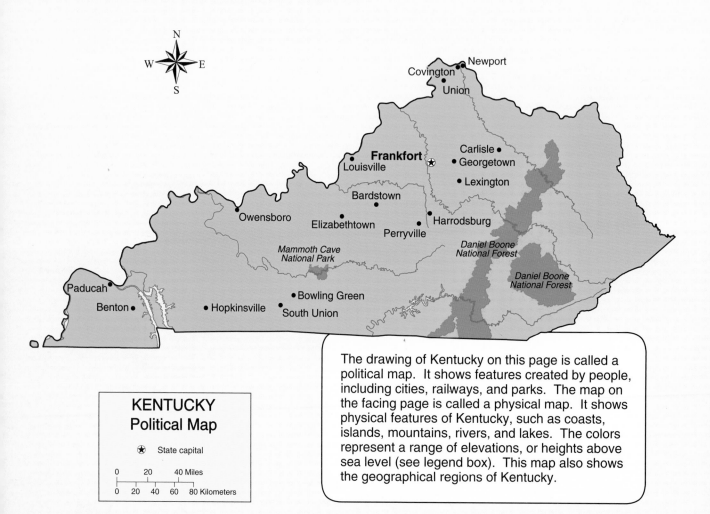

KENTUCKY
Political Map

⊛ State capital

```
0        20        40 Miles
0   20   40   60   80 Kilometers
```

The drawing of Kentucky on this page is called a political map. It shows features created by people, including cities, railways, and parks. The map on the facing page is called a physical map. It shows physical features of Kentucky, such as coasts, islands, mountains, rivers, and lakes. The colors represent a range of elevations, or heights above sea level (see legend box). This map also shows the geographical regions of Kentucky.

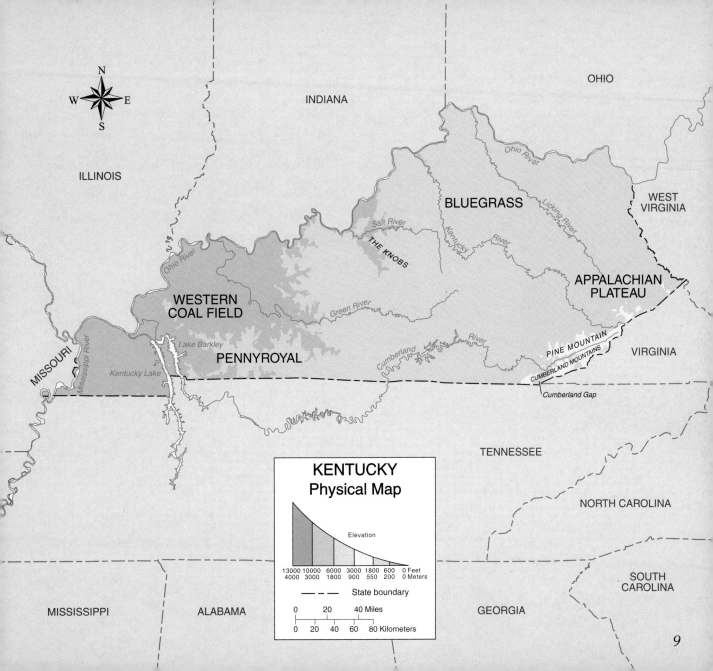

OHIO

INDIANA

ILLINOIS

WEST
VIRGINIA

BLUEGRASS

Ohio River

Licking River

Salt River

THE KNOBS

Ohio River

Kentucky River

**APPALACHIAN
PLATEAU**

**WESTERN
COAL FIELD**

Green River

Mississippi River

Lake Barkley

PENNYROYAL

Cumberland River

River

PINE MOUNTAIN

VIRGINIA

CUMBERLAND MOUNTAINS

MISSOURI

Kentucky Lake

Cumberland Gap

TENNESSEE

NORTH CAROLINA

KENTUCKY
Physical Map

Elevation

| 13000 | 10000 | 6000 | 3000 | 1800 | 600 | 0 Feet |
| 4000 | 3000 | 1800 | 900 | 550 | 200 | 0 Meters |

– – – – State boundary

| 0 | 20 | 40 Miles |

| 0 | 20 | 40 | 60 | 80 Kilometers |

MISSISSIPPI

ALABAMA

GEORGIA

SOUTH
CAROLINA

9

Cypress trees grow in the wet swamps of western Kentucky.

Boone and other settlers found more than open land in Kentucky. They also found giant caves, hardwood forests, tree-studded mountains, and wide rivers. Rivers form more than half of the state's boundaries. Beyond the borders lie Kentucky's neighboring states—Virginia and West Virginia to the west; Ohio, Indiana, and Illinois to the north; Missouri to the east; and Tennessee to the south.

Kentucky's fertile land was formed millions of years ago, when an ancient sea flooded much of the state. Coral, shellfish, and sharks lived in the invading waters. When the ocean dried up, it left behind the shells and skeletons of the sea creatures. Over time their remains decayed into a rich soil.

Another valuable resource developed in the ancient **swamps** that covered eastern and western Kentucky. Swampland plants died and began to rot. Layers of heavy soil collected above the decaying plants. Over millions of years, as the weight of the soil pressed them together, the plants changed into coal, a black substance used as a fuel.

Coal deposits and fertile soil are only two of Kentucky's riches. The state's four land regions each have their own features and natural resources. In the east is the mountainous Appalachian Plateau. The tree-covered peaks of the Pine Mountains rise from the **plateau,** an area of high, flat land. Many steep valleys, rushing rivers, and winding streams cut through the region. One of Kentucky's two major coal deposits, the Eastern Coal Field, lies beneath part of the Appalachian Plateau.

Lush forests blanket the Appalachian Plateau, which covers more than one-fourth of the state.

Kentucky's famous bluegrass and tobacco grow in the Bluegrass Region of north central Kentucky. Long wooden fences stretch across the area's grassy hills and mark the borders of horse farms. Sandy, conelike formations called **knobs** lie along the southern edge of the Bluegrass Region. This area is known as the Knobs.

Horse farms are a common sight in the Bluegrass Region.

Running water carved Mammoth Cave out of limestone underneath the Pennyroyal Region.

The Pennyroyal Region sprawls along much of Kentucky's southern border, reaching north to the Knobs and west to Missouri. A barren area separates the Pennyroyal's flat farm-land in the south from its rocky ridges and bluffs in the north. Cypress swamps cover the western corner of the region.

The Western Coal Field lies in northwestern Kentucky. The region is surrounded on three sides by the Pennyroyal. About half of Kentucky's plentiful coal reserves are buried under the steep hills and fertile soil of the Western Coal Field.

The jagged Ohio River separates Kentucky from Ohio. The historic town of Maysville, Kentucky, lies along this path.

Water is an abundant natural resource in Kentucky. In fact, Kentucky claims more miles of running water than any other state except Alaska. Ships travel on more than 1,000 miles of these rivers, which serve as trade routes. Some of the most important rivers are the Ohio, the Mississippi, the Green, the Kentucky, the Licking, and the Salt.

Of the many lakes scattered throughout Kentucky, some of the largest are artificial, formed by huge dams built on rivers. Besides creating lakes, dams help control water. They hold back rivers to keep them from overflowing after heavy rains. Dams create energy for Kentucky, too. When released through a dam, the river water creates a strong force, which turns giant engines that produce electricity.

Plentiful rain fills the rivers and lakes of Kentucky and nourishes its crops and plant life. About 48 inches of rain falls in the state each year, mostly during the spring.

Although Kentucky's weather is generally mild, the state has four distinct seasons. Winter is cool and moist, with a few light snowfalls. Usually the temperature stays above freezing, except in the mountains of the southeast. Summers in Kentucky are hot and humid, with temperatures averaging 77° F. Thunderstorms, and sometimes tornadoes, blow through the state in the spring and summer.

Winter can bring beautiful snowfalls to parts of Kentucky, such as this creek near Louisville.

In the spring, dogwoods *(right)* bloom over much of the state. Barn owls *(below)* make their homes in hollow trees and empty buildings throughout Kentucky.

The state's rainy weather and rich soil provide the perfect environment for a wide variety of plant life. Thick forests of ash, beech, hickory, and oak blanket almost half of the state. Many flowering trees, such as the fragrant magnolia, are also found in Kentucky.

Deer abound in Kentucky's forests. Foxes, skunks, and mink also prowl in wooded areas, while raccoon, chipmunks, and opossums raise their young in fields, in forests, and even in city neighborhoods.

Blazing a Trail

 entucky's earliest inhabitants hunted mammoths and mastodons, huge hairy elephants with great tusks and giant teeth. The ancestors of these hunters probably found their way to North America while following prey across the Bering Strait, a land bridge that once connected North America to Asia.

The hunters reached Kentucky about 12,000 years ago. As the weather got drier and big game animals died out, the Native Americans, or Indians, hunted smaller animals and gathered seeds, nuts, and fruits for food.

Fog settles over the Appalachian Mountains in Cumberland Gap National Historical Park.

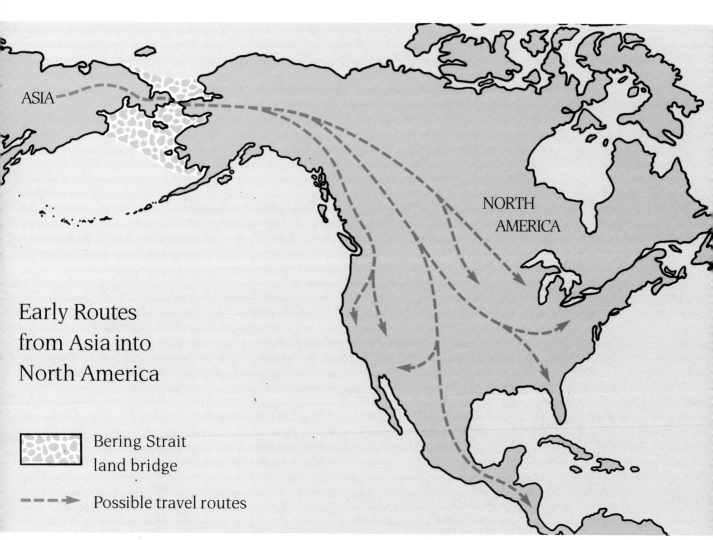

ASIA

NORTH
AMERICA

Early Routes
from Asia into
North America

Bering Strait
land bridge

- - - ▶ Possible travel routes

The Indians who came to the Kentucky area were probably descendants of Indians who
traveled on foot from Asia.

Some of these Indians stopped moving from place to place and settled in the north central part of Kentucky about 2,500 years ago. Called mound builders, they buried their dead in pits or tombs. Important people were buried with treasured objects, such as pottery. The Indians piled layer upon layer of dirt on top of the tombs, creating large mounds.

Using wood, mud, and grasses, the mound builders also built villages. They planted corn, beans, and squash to feed large populations. But by the early 1500s, the mound builders had disappeared. No one is sure what happened to them. Their crops may have failed because the weather became too dry or too cold.

A mound builder standing on a temple mound worships a god. Some of these Indians made temple mounds as well as burial mounds.

The Woodland Indians were the next group to move to the area. Like the mound builders, these Indians were farmers. They built villages along Kentucky's many rivers.

But when the first Europeans ventured into the area in the 1600s, they found no Indian villages. The early Woodland Indians had moved away, and Kentucky had become a hunting ground shared by the Shawnee, Cherokee, and Iroquois Indians.

In 1750 Thomas Walker, an explorer, left his home in Virginia (one of the 13 British **colonies** in North America). He crossed into what would become

Kentucky's rivers provided plenty of fish for Woodland Indians.

When Daniel Boone visited Kentucky for the second time, he brought a hunting party from North Carolina. For two years, these men lived in Kentucky's wilderness.

eastern Kentucky through a low place, called a pass, in the Cumberland Mountains. Walker named the pass the Cumberland Gap. In 1774 James Harrod and a group of colonists followed Walker's path through the gap and established Harrodsburg, the first permanent white settlement in the area.

Not long afterward, Daniel Boone blazed a trail through the mountain forests of the Cumberland Gap. This path came to be called the Wilderness Road. Hundreds of people from the 13 colonies made their way west—to Kentucky and beyond—on that trail. The pioneers were looking for more land on which to build homes and farms.

To protect themselves against Indian attacks, Kentucky's earliest pioneers built thick log walls around their settlements.

The Shawnee and the Cherokee did not trust most of these pioneers. Most settlers showed little respect for the Indians and their hunting grounds. Fearful that the newcomers would take over the area, the Shawnee and Cherokee became hostile toward the settlers.

The Indians and the settlers battled each other fiercely for the land. The Indians got many of their guns from the British, who were fighting the colonists in a war called the American Revolution (1775–1783). Armies of Indians, led by British commanders, fought against groups of settlers at Kentucky forts such as Boonesborough and Fort Harrod.

The colonists defeated the British in 1783 and formed their own country—the United States of America. Kentucky became a county, or section, of the state of Virginia.

During the American Revolution, British leaders met with Indians to convince them to join their fight against the colonists.

Virginians traveled through the wild Cumberland Gap on their way to Kentucky County, where they hoped to establish new homes.

Virginia encouraged people to move to its western land. Between 1783 and the early 1790s, almost 100,000 people traveled the Wilderness Road through the Cumberland Gap to reach Kentucky County. The county soon had enough people to apply for statehood, and by 1792 Kentucky had become the 15th state to join the Union.

The Shawnee and Cherokee still fought to regain their land, but more settlers kept coming. By 1794 the U.S. Army had pushed the Shawnee west to what would become Missouri, and the Cherokee south to Tennessee and North Carolina. Few Indians remained in Kentucky.

Kentucky's rich farmland attracted more and more settlers. By 1800 the state's population had grown to 200,000 people. About one-fifth of these people were African slaves. Settlers from southern states brought the slaves to Kentucky to work in tobacco and corn fields.

Most Kentuckians made a living from farming. Farmers used river routes to transport their products to market. Crops and livestock were shipped from Kentucky to ports along the Mississippi and Ohio Rivers.

Before settlers could build homes or plant crops in Kentucky, they had to cut down thick forests.

In 1829 Kentuckians opened a waterway from Kentucky to New Orleans, Louisiana, by building a canal around the Falls of the Ohio River. The waterway allowed steamboats to carry Kentucky's hemp, tobacco, and bourbon to markets along the Mississippi.

By 1840 Kentucky led the nation in the growing of hemp, a plant used to make rope. By 1860 Kentucky was growing more tobacco than any other state. When bourbon, a type of alcohol made from corn and invented in Kentucky, became popular among settlers, Kentuckians began growing more corn, too.

In 1860 most people who lived in the southern United States were farmers. Some of them used slaves to raise crops in order to make a profit.

Factories were more common than farms in the North, where more people lived in cities and did not rely on slave labor.

Kentucky had strong ties to both the North and South. Like Southerners, almost all Kentuckians still lived in the countryside and farmed the land. But like many Northerners, many Kentuckians were opposed to slavery.

When Northerners began pushing Southerners to outlaw slavery, several Southern states decided to form a separate country that allowed slavery. They called their new nation the Confederate States of America. Kentuckians were torn. Should they join this new country with their Southern neighbors or stay in the Union with their Northern neighbors?

Kentuckians didn't want to choose sides in this conflict, which became known as the Civil War (1861–1865). But when both Union (Northern) and Confederate (Southern) troops invaded the state in 1861, Kentucky's government decided to stay in the Union. The state government forced Confederate troops to leave Kentucky.

In 1862 Confederate and Union troops fought for control of Kentucky in the Battle of Perryville. After the Confederates lost, they returned to their camps in Tennessee.

Still, many Kentuckians felt loyal to the South, and 35,000 of them fought for the Confederacy. More than twice as many Kentuckians fought for the North. When the Union won the war in 1865, however, it treated Kentucky as a defeated enemy. Union troops were sent to occupy sections of the state that had sided with the South.

Kentucky was heavily damaged by the war. Homes, crops, and livestock had been lost in battles. Army troops had destroyed most of the state's transportation systems and nearly all of its schools.

Some Kentuckians joined a group called the Ku Klux Klan after the Civil War. The Klan attacked black people and Union supporters, sometimes beating them or setting their homes on fire.

The Hatfields and the McCoys

During the Civil War, friends, neighbors, and family members in Kentucky sometimes fought on opposite sides. This occasionally caused feuds, or fights, that lasted long after the war ended. One of the state's most famous feuds was between the McCoys from Kentucky and the Hatfields who lived in nearby West Virginia.

Over the years, many stories have been told about the feuding. One tale says that the trouble began in 1863 when a soldier from the pro-Union McCoy family was found dead near the Hatfields' home. The McCoys thought that the Hatfields, who were Confederates, had killed the soldier.

To get even, the McCoys killed a Hatfield.

The fighting grew worse in 1882, when a Hatfield man and a McCoy woman tried to elope, or run away to get married secretly. Their families caught them. In the battle that followed, a Hatfield was shot. Later, three McCoy brothers were found murdered.

A small-scale war between the families followed. At least 20 and possibly as many as 100 people were killed before the feuding ended in the 1890s. Since that time, the two families have made amends. Each summer they get together for a Hatfield-McCoy reunion.

Kentuckians labored to rebuild their state. Farmers replanted their fields, while shopkeepers restocked their stores. Kentucky's traders went to the South, where people had suffered even more losses in the war and needed Kentucky's goods and crops.

Crops, coal, and manufactured goods were transported from Kentucky to markets in the South on the Louisville and Nashville Railroad.

In the mid-1800s, Kentucky produced almost all of the nation's hemp.

Coal production, like trade, increased steadily after the Civil War. Throughout the country, thousands of factories were built, and they needed coal to run their machinery. Kentucky began producing more coal than almost any other state.

Tobacco continued to be an important source of money for Kentucky, gradually replacing hemp as the number-one crop. Louisville became the world's largest tobacco market, with traders buying and selling tobacco leaves and tobacco products.

In the early 1900s, most Kentuckians still lived on small farms. Farm families raised most of their own food. Hunting and fishing added meat to the family table.

The Black Patch War

In the early 1900s, Kentucky's farmers grew more tobacco than farmers in almost any other state. Big tobacco companies made lots of money selling tobacco products, such as cigarettes and cigars, nationwide. But the American Tobacco Company of Kentucky wanted to make even more money. The company started to offer farmers low prices for their tobacco crops. Before long, American Tobacco convinced other companies to bid the same low rate.

Angry farmers in southwestern Kentucky banded together and refused to sell their tobacco so cheaply. Some farmers, however, continued to sell tobacco for the low price. They said they couldn't afford to stop selling their crops altogether.

To stop these tobacco sales, a group of farmers formed the Night Riders in 1904. For the next four years, the riders went out after dark to burn the fields and barns of the farmers who kept selling their crops.

These raids became known as the Black Patch War because the Night Riders grew dark-leafed tobacco. Kentucky's government sent army troops to the area in 1909 and stopped the Night Riders. But the farmers won—companies began to pay higher tobacco prices once again.

During World War I, many Kentuckians left their farms to earn more money as coal miners. But mining was dangerous work. Almost all miners developed lung diseases from breathing coal dust, and many miners died in accidents.

World War I (1914–1918) changed the lives of Kentucky's farmers. The war created a high demand for coal, which fueled the factories that made weapons. Mining towns sprang up near Kentucky's coal fields as farmers left their homes to dig for the mineral. But the mining boom ended with the war. Most miners, who had sold their farms to work in the mines, lost their jobs and their only source of money.

In 1937 one of the worst floods ever recorded on the Ohio River happened. It caused great damage to cities all along the river's banks. The flood left nearly a million people homeless, and schools were closed for more than a month.

More people lost their jobs in the 1930s, during a period called the Great Depression. Many banks and businesses shut down. But during World War II (1939–1945), coal was needed once more, and mining again employed thousands of Kentuckians. Meanwhile, new factories were being built in Louisville and Lexington, creating jobs for the rural Kentuckians who were moving to the cities.

Tobacco warehouses in Louisville and Lexington supplied jobs for many Kentuckians. Workers either bundled the leaves for sale or sold them to tobacco companies.

At the same time, the state began to change the way it treated African Americans. Black people in many states, including Kentucky, had not been allowed to go to the same schools or hospitals as white people. Many businesses hired only white workers.

During the 1950s and 1960s, African Americans protested the way they were being treated and demonstrated for their **civil rights,** or personal freedoms. In 1966 Kentucky became the first southern state to pass a law that said employers could not refuse to hire workers because of the color of their skin.

During some civil rights protests, troops in Kentucky guarded the streets of Louisville.

In 1990 Kentuckians voted to improve the state's educational system.

By 1970, for the first time in the state's history, more Kentuckians were living in cities and towns than in rural areas. This was an important change, but many other changes have also shaped Kentucky.

A big focus for the state has been improving its public school system. In the 1990s, the state adopted a plan to reform its schools in both rural areas and cities. Kentucky has also worked hard to strengthen its economy by attracting new businesses to the state.

Native Americans no longer hunt mammoths, and pioneers no longer travel the Wilderness Road. The first trails marked in Kentucky have grown old, but Kentuckians keep blazing new trails.

PEOPLE & ECONOMY

City Life and Fertile Farmland

hough Kentucky still has the bluegrass fields and rolling mountains Daniel Boone loved, he probably wouldn't want to live in the state today. According to Boone, elbow room meant not being able to see the smoke from his neighbors' chimneys. Kentucky's population has grown so much that Boone would have lots of trouble finding that kind of elbow room.

Kentucky's rural areas are much more populated than they once were.

More than 4 million people call Kentucky home. About half of them live in urban areas, or cities. Kentucky's largest urban center is Lexington-Fayette, followed by Louisville, Owensboro, Bowling Green, and Covington. Except for Lexington and Bowling Green, all of these cities lie along the southern bank of the Ohio River.

Most Kentuckians have ancestors who came from England, Scotland, Ireland, France, or Germany. About 7 percent of the state's population is African American. People from Central and South American countries make up an even smaller part of Kentucky's population—about 1.5 percent. Small numbers of Native Americans and Asian Americans also make Kentucky their home.

Kentuckians are famous for many things, especially racehorses. Many people in the state make a living by raising and selling Thoroughbreds, a breed of horse that is well-suited to racing. In the Bluegrass Region, horse lovers can stroll through horse farms, ride ponies at the Kentucky Horse Park, or watch the races at the Keeneland Race

Course in Lexington. The Kentucky Derby, a horse race that has been run on Louisville's Churchill Downs since 1875, draws thousands of onlookers every May.

Racehorses burst out of the gate at the Keeneland Race Course.

Kentucky is also known for its bluegrass music. Banjos, fiddles, harmonicas, and mandolins are common bluegrass instruments. Kentuckian Bill Monroe and his Blue Grass Boys first performed this folk music just before World War II. Since then bluegrass bands have entertained people at festivals and celebrations all over the state.

Kentucky has large national forests and state parks that draw many visitors to the state each year. Some visitors hike through Daniel Boone National Forest. Others ride down the Big South Fork of the Cumberland River on rafts. Tourists can also visit historic forts and homes, such as Old Fort Harrod at Harrodsburg—Kentucky's oldest town.

A mandolin player entertains his audience with a bluegrass tune.

Canoeists explore this
Kentucky creek.

With more than 300 miles of passages, Mammoth
Cave in central Kentucky is part of the world's
longest cave system. Here, visitors can tour the
huge underground caverns of Crystal Lake, have
lunch in the Snowball Dining Room, or squeeze
through the narrow passages of Fat Man's Misery.
On one tour, visitors can even float in a boat down
the underground Echo River.

Rain showers do not keep the audience away from the Festival of the Bluegrass in Lexington.

Louisville, one of the state's cultural centers, offers an orchestra, a ballet, an opera, and the nationally famous Actors Theater. Lexington has its own orchestra and holds a bluegrass music festival every summer.

As basketball fans around the country know, Louisville and Lexington are home to rival college basketball teams. The University of Louisville's Cardinals and the University of Kentucky's Wildcats draw large crowds from around the state. Kentucky's baseball fans cheer for the Louisville Bats, a minor-league baseball team.

Night falls on a Louisville Bats game at Slugger Field in Louisville.

More than half of Kentucky's workers—about 57 percent—have service jobs helping people or businesses. Some of these workers are nurses, lawyers, or bank tellers. Others sell clothes, food, or cars.

About 15 percent of Kentucky's workforce works for the government. Two military bases, Forts Knox and Campbell, employ thousands of soldiers and other workers.

Service workers in Kentucky do all kinds of jobs, from helping tourists at resorts *(above)* to transporting coal *(right)*.

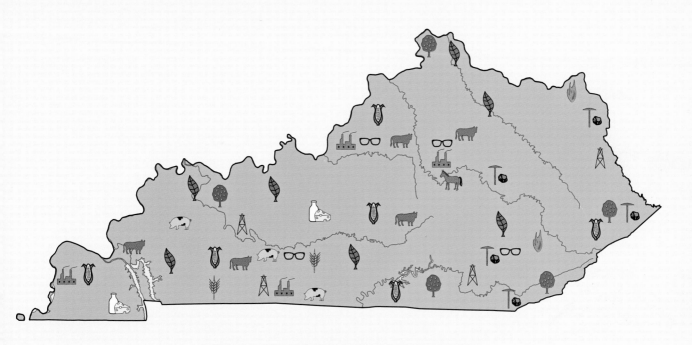

KENTUCKY
Economic Map

The symbols on this map show where different economic activities take place in Kentucky. The legend below explains what each symbol stands for.

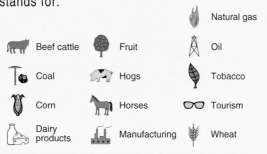

		Natural gas
Beef cattle	Fruit	Oil
Coal	Hogs	Tobacco
Corn	Horses	Tourism
Dairy products	Manufacturing	Wheat

Generations of Kentuckians have aged bourbon in oak barrels.

Coal and oil, found in the Eastern and Western Coal Fields, are the state's most valuable minerals. Although only about 1 percent of Kentuckians work in mining, this industry brings in 3 percent of all the state's money.

Nearly 30 percent of all money earned in Kentucky comes from manufacturing. Workers make a lot of bourbon, a whiskey named after a county in central Kentucky. In fact, Kentucky makes more bourbon than any other state. Louisville is a leading processor of tobacco. People make the dried tobacco leaves into cigarettes and other tobacco products. Workers in the state also make tractors, cars and trucks, medicines, paint, air conditioners, and typewriters.

Some Kentuckians work in car factories.

Right: Tobacco earns more money for Kentuckians than any other crop. *Below:* A soldier shows off his helmet to a friend, who might someday become a soldier, too.

Tobacco, of course, grows on many of Kentucky's farms. Besides tobacco, farmers harvest soybeans, corn, and wheat. Others breed horses or raise cattle. Kentuckians also enjoy home-grown apples, peaches, and the famous popcorn of Calloway County.

Despite its many farms, Kentucky is no longer mainly a farming state. Agriculture employs only 6 percent of the state's workers. Kentucky still has miles of rich farmland, but its people can choose from many different kinds of work.

THE ENVIRONMENT

Surface Mining

Kentucky has many valuable natural resources, including water and soil. But one of the state's most profitable natural resources is coal. Kentucky's coal miners earned more than $830 million in 1998. That same year, the state produced about 157 million tons of coal.

More than one-third of Kentucky's coal is uncovered by **surface mining.** Surface miners scrape or blast off the tops of hills and mountains to expose the coal underneath. They strip away trees and topsoil, leaving ugly scars in the land.

About 1 percent of Kentucky's workers are employed in mining.

Surface mining not only destroys the beauty of the land but also ruins farmland and pollutes rivers and streams. By removing the trees and plants that protect the soil, surface mining also causes **erosion.** In this process, wind and rain carry the exposed soil around the mine into clear streams, turning the streams to mud. Erosion can also cause landslides that destroy homes and more land.

One form of mining in Kentucky is called surface mining. Surface miners cut rock, soil, and trees from hills to reach Kentucky's coal.

Until 1977 few laws protected the land from the effects of surface mining. But the Surface Mining Control and Reclamation Act of 1977 changed that. The law requires that owners of surface mines practice **reclamation.** This means they must reclaim, or restore, land damaged by surface mines. To do this, mine owners put soil back onto the mine, plant trees and grasses, and leave the land at least as useful as it was before mining began.

At abandoned mines, acid can collect in pools of water. The acidic water is carried by rain into nearby streams and rivers, where the acid kills fish and plants.

To make sure that miners follow the law, the state government charges mine operators a fee before they begin mining. Mine operators get that money back once they have completed the mining and have reclaimed the stripped land. If an operator does not do a good job of restoring the mine, the government keeps the fee and uses that money to rebuild the stripped area.

As part of the reclamation process, miners replant mined land with trees and flowers.

Wildcatters strip the soil off a coal mine.

Government inspectors try to make sure that everyone follows the reclamation laws, but surface mining remains a problem. The law does not require surface mines dug before 1977 to be reclaimed. And until 1987, surface mines of two acres or less didn't have to be reclaimed either.

Reclamation can be expensive, and many mine operators do not want to pay for it. To avoid paying for reclamation, some people operate small, hidden mines in Kentucky. These miners, called **wildcatters,** secretly mine coal and then leave the area without rebuilding the stripped land.

Wildcatters mine coal *(opposite page)*. To avoid being spied on by surface-mining inspectors, the miners hide their bulldozers in nearby forests *(above)*.

Surface-mining inspectors fly over coal fields in helicopters looking for wildcatters, but illegal mining still occurs in Kentucky. When inspectors find illegal mines, the wildcatters are brought to court. But in some cases, they avoid paying fines.

Local judges and juries sometimes choose not to enforce the reclamation laws. The courts know that

some wildcatters turn to illegal mining because they
can't find any other work. And once the damage
to the land is done, many wildcatters claim they
cannot afford to reclaim the land they have mined.
So the wildcatters go free.

To reclaim land, miners use the soil they removed from the mine to fill in nearby valleys and turn the stripped landscape into farmland. In this way, the reclaimed land can become as useful as it was before it was mined.

But the state is making progress. By 2000 a national award for surface-mining reclamation had been given to one Kentucky company for four years in a row. Many mining companies do an excellent job of restoring the land. The state's Department for Surface Mining Reclamation and Enforcement is hard at work repairing old mine sites and stopping further damage. Kentucky's coal deposits are expected to last another 200 years, so reclaiming mine sites will be an important job for years to come.

On reclaimed coal mines, trees and other plants replace bare soil.

ALL ABOUT KENTUCKY

Fun Facts

Billions of dollars worth of gold are held in the underground vaults of Fort Knox, Kentucky. The door to the main vault is made of concrete and steel and weighs more than 20 tons.

The country's first cheeseburger was served in 1934 at Kaelin's Restaurant in Louisville, Kentucky.

The public saw an electric light for the first time in Louisville. Thomas Edison introduced his light bulb to crowds at the Southern Exposition in 1883.

A rainbow makes a colorful arc over Cumberland Falls. Moonlight sometimes creates a similar arc at night.

If you visited Mammoth Cave National Park in Kentucky, you would be in the longest known cave system in the world. The cave has over 300 miles of mapped trails.

When the moon is full, a moonbow appears in the mist created by Cumberland Falls in Kentucky. This nighttime display of colors has been seen nowhere else in the western half of the world.

STATE SONG

MY OLD KENTUCKY HOME

Words and music by Stephen C. Foster

You can hear "My Old Kentucky Home" by visiting the following
website and scrolling down to the State Song link:
<http://www.state.ky.us/agencies/gov/symbols.htm>

A KENTUCKY RECIPE

When European settlers arrived in
Kentucky hundreds of years ago,
Native Americans were already
using popcorn as both a snack
and decoration. Kentucky has
since become famous for the popping
corn it grows. This sweet and chewy
popcorn recipe is easy to make and delicious to
eat. Ask an adult to help you with all steps using a stove.

POPCORN MARSHMALLOW BALLS

1 tablespoon vegetable oil   ½ cup butter
5 cups miniature marshmallows   ½ cup popping corn

1. Grease a 9- x 13-inch baking dish.
2. Pour vegetable oil in a 4-quart saucepan and heat on high.
3. When oil is hot, add popping corn. Move pan constantly.
4. When finished popping, remove popcorn from heat and place in
   greased baking dish.
5. Melt butter in a medium pan on low heat.
6. Add marshmallows to butter and stir until melted.
7. Pour marshmallows over popcorn and mix with spoon. Make sure
   popcorn gets coated evenly.
8. Let mixture cool slightly.
9. Smear butter or non-stick cooking spray on hands.
10. With hands, form popcorn into 8 balls. Enjoy!

HISTORICAL TIMELINE

10,000 B.C. Native American hunters reach what later became Kentucky.

500 B.C. Mound builders arrive in Kentucky and build villages.

A.D. 1500 Woodland Indians begin farming near the Ohio River.

1750 Thomas Walker explores Kentucky and discovers the Cumberland Gap.

1774 Harrodsburg, the first permanent white settlement in the Kentucky area, is founded.

1775 Daniel Boone leads the blazing of the Wilderness Road; the American Revolution (1775–1883) begins.

1792 Kentucky becomes the 15th state.

1794 Most Shawnee and Cherokee Indians have been pushed out of Kentucky by the U.S. Army.

1860 Kentucky becomes the nation's leading tobacco grower.

1861 Kentucky remains in the Union as the Civil War (1861–1865) begins.

1882 A small-scale war breaks out between the Hatfields and the McCoys.

1904–1909 The Black Patch War over tobacco prices takes place in Kentucky.

1917 The United States enters World War I (1914–1918), creating a greater demand for Kentucky's coal.

1929 The Great Depression begins, leading to a decline in Kentucky's economy.

1941 The United States enters World War II (1939–1945), which produces new jobs for workers in Kentucky.

1970 More Kentuckians live in urban areas than in rural areas.

1977 The Surface Mining Control and Reclamation Act is passed.

1990 The Kentucky Education Reform Act is passed to improve the state's schools.

2000 For the fourth year in a row, a Kentucky company receives the Excellence in Surface Coal Mining Reclamation award.

OUTSTANDING KENTUCKIANS

Muhammad
Ali

Muhammad Ali (Cassius Clay) (born 1942), from Louisville, first became the Heavyweight Boxing Champion of the World in 1964, after only 20 fights. He earned the same title two more times before retiring in 1979.

Daniel Boone (1734–1820) first saw Kentucky on a hunting trip. He returned with other pioneers and built Boonesborough—one of Kentucky's first white settlements. Although Boone died in Missouri, he is buried in Frankfort, Kentucky.

Daniel Boone

Mary Breckinridge (1881–1965) moved to Leslie County, Kentucky, in the 1920s. She created the Frontier Nursing Services, a group of health care clinics that brought improved health care services to rural mountain families.

Cassius Marcellus Clay (1810–1903), of Madison County, Kentucky, was an antislavery activist and politician. He served in the Kentucky legislature and founded an antislavery paper, the *True American*.

Mary
Breckinridge

Henry Clay (1777–1852) began his political career in the Kentucky state legislature in 1803. He then served in the U.S. Senate and as the U.S. secretary of state. He was known as the Great Compromiser for his skill at settling arguments.

Jefferson Davis (1808–1889), from Todd County, was president of the Confederate States of America during the Civil War. Before the war began, he had been a member of Congress and then secretary of war for the United States.

Henry Clay

Red Foley (1910–1968), of Bluelick, Kentucky, has been called the founder of country music. Some of his hits were "Smoke on the Water," "Chattanoogie Shoe Shine Boy," and "Peace in the Valley." Foley was made a member of the Country Music Hall of Fame in 1967.

Crystal Gayle

Crystal Gayle (born 1951) is a country music singer from Paintsville, Kentucky. The sister of Loretta Lynn, Gayle won a Grammy Award for her song "Don't It Make My Brown Eyes Blue."

Duncan Hines (1880–1959) was born in Bowling Green, Kentucky. From 1936 to 1959, he wrote national restaurant guidebooks called *Adventures in Good Eating*. He later gained more fame when his name became a brand name for packaged foods.

Duncan Hines

Naomi Judd (born 1946) and **Wynonna Judd** (born 1964) from Ashland, Kentucky, found success together in the 1980s and 1990s as a mother-daughter singing team. The Judds won many music awards, including five Grammys. They also won over millions of fans with songs such as "Mama He's Crazy," "Give a Little Love," and "Love Can Build a Bridge." In the early 1990s, Naomi became too ill to perform. Since then, Wynonna has pursued a career as an award-winning solo artist.

Wynonna Judd

Abraham Lincoln (1809–1865) was born near what became Hodgenville, Kentucky. In 1861 he became the 16th U.S. president. During his time in office, Lincoln issued the Emancipation Proclamation, which eventually led to the end of slavery in the United States.

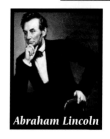

Abraham Lincoln

Loretta Lynn

Loretta Lynn (born 1935) is a country music singer from Butcher Hollow, Kentucky. Lynn was the first woman to receive the Entertainer of the Year award from the Country Music Association. Lynn has recorded many hit songs, including "Coal Miner's Daughter." Her autobiography of the same name was made into a movie.

George Ella Lyon (born 1949) grew up in Harlan, Kentucky—a mountain coal town that probably gave her ideas for her children's books. Some of her books include *Red Rover, Red Rover; Borrowed Children; Come a Tide;* and *With a Hammer for My Heart.*

Bill Monroe

Bill Monroe (1911–1996) is known as the father of bluegrass music. His hits include "Blue Moon of Kentucky," "Linda Lou," and "Uncle Pen." Monroe was inducted into the Country Music Hall of Fame in 1970. He was born near Rosine, Kentucky.

Pee Wee Reese

Harold Henry "Pee Wee" Reese (1918–1999) played shortstop for the Brooklyn Dodgers in the 1940s and 1950s. He had a large role in the acceptance of teammate Jackie Robinson as the first black man to play major-league baseball. Reese, from Elkton, Kentucky, was elected to the National Baseball Hall of Fame in 1984.

Colonel Harland Sanders

Colonel Harland Sanders (1890–1980), owner of Sanders' Café in Corbin, Kentucky, founded Kentucky Fried Chicken, a fast-food restaurant, in the 1950s. Sanders was made an honorary colonel by the governor of Kentucky in 1935.

Diane Sawyer (born 1945) is a television journalist. Born in Glasgow, Kentucky, Sawyer was the first female reporter on *60 Minutes.* She co-hosts two television news shows—*Prime Time Live* and *Good Morning America.*

Seabiscuit (1933–1947) was one of the most successful racehorses of all time. Born on Claiborne Farm in Paris, Kentucky, Seabiscuit went on to beat top racehorses and claim Horse of the Year honors in 1938. When he stopped racing a year later, he had won 33 races out of 89 starts, a U.S. Thoroughbred record at the time.

Seabiscuit

Zachary Taylor (1784–1850), who grew up near Louisville, served as the 12th U.S. president from 1849 to 1850. Nicknamed Old Rough-and-Ready, Taylor became a national war hero when he fought in the Mexican-American War (1846–1848).

Zachary Taylor

Jim Varney (1949–2000) was an actor and comedian from Lexington. He began his career making commercials and played the part of Ernest in the motion pictures *Ernest Saves Christmas* and *Ernest Goes to Camp.*

Robert Penn Warren (1905–1989) was a novelist, poet, teacher, and literary critic from Guthrie, Kentucky. He won three Pulitzer Prizes and earned the title poet laureate, or outstanding poet, of the United States in 1986.

Enid Yandell

Enid Yandell (1870–1934), a sculptor, was born in Louisville. Her works of art are displayed throughout Kentucky and other states. Some of her famous works include the Carrie Brown Memorial Fountain, the Emma Willard Memorial, and "The Five Senses" sculpture. Yandell was the first female member of the National Sculpture Society.

Whitney Moore Young Jr.

Whitney Moore Young Jr. (1921–1971), born in Lincoln Ridge, Kentucky, was a civil rights leader. Young worked to get job training, quality education, and decent housing for black people. He was the director of the National Urban League from 1961 to 1971.

FACTS-AT-A-GLANCE

Nickname: Bluegrass State

Song: "My Old Kentucky Home"

Motto: United We Stand, Divided We Fall

Flower: goldenrod

Tree: tulip tree

Bird: Kentucky cardinal

Horse: Thoroughbred

Fish: Kentucky bass

Fossil: brachiopod

Rock: Kentucky agate

Date and ranking of statehood: June 1, 1792, the 15th state

Capital: Frankfort

Area: 39,732 square miles

Rank in area, nationwide: 36th

Average January temperature: 34° F

Average July temperature: 77° F

The pioneer and the politician on Kentucky's flag represent the people who worked to make Kentucky a state. The flag pictured was made official in 1962.

POPULATION GROWTH

Millions

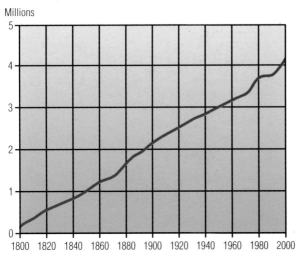

This chart shows how Kentucky's population has grown from 1800 to 2000.

A statesman and a frontiersman stand together, surrounded by Kentucky's motto, *United We Stand, Divided We Fall.* A wreath of goldenrod, the state flower, rests at the bottom of the seal.

Population: 4,041,769 (2000 census)

Rank in population, nationwide: 25th

Major cities and populations (2000 census): Lexington-Fayette (260,512), Louisville (256,231), Owensboro (54,067), Bowling Green (49,296), Covington (43,370), Frankfort (27,741)

U.S. senators: 2

U.S. representatives: 6

Electoral votes: 8

Natural resources: clays, coal, fertile fluorite, lakes and rivers, lead, limestone, natural gas, petroleum, sand and gravel, soil

Agricultural products: apples, beef, corn, hogs, milk, peaches, popcorn, soybeans, Thoroughbred horses, tobacco, wheat

Manufactured goods: air conditioners, bourbon whiskey, cars, medicines, paint, tobacco products, tractors, typewriters

WHERE KENTUCKIANS WORK

Services—57 percent (services includes jobs in trade; community, social, and personal services; finance, insurance, and real estate; transportation, communication, and utilities)

Manufacturing—15 percent

Government—15 percent

Construction—6 percent

Agriculture—6 percent

Mining—1 percent

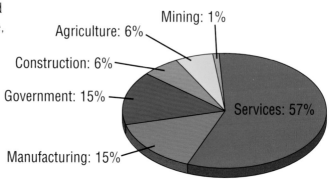

Mining: 1%

Agriculture: 6%

Construction: 6%

Government: 15%

Manufacturing: 15%

Services: 57%

GROSS STATE PRODUCT

Services—49 percent

Manufacturing—28 percent

Government—13 percent

Construction—4 percent

Agriculture—3 percent

Mining—3 percent

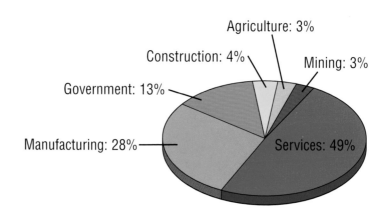

Agriculture: 3%

Construction: 4%

Mining: 3%

Government: 13%

Manufacturing: 28%

Services: 49%

WILDLIFE

Mammals: chipmunk, fox, mink, muskrat, opossum, rabbit, raccoon, squirrel, woodchuck

Birds: cardinal, crow, dove, egret, grackle, grouse, heron, quail, wild duck, wild goose, woodpecker

Reptiles and amphibians: copperhead, frog, lizard, rattlesnake, skink, toad, treefrog, turtle

Fish: bass, bluegill, buffalo fish, carp, catfish, muskellunge, rockfish, shad, walleye

Trees: ash, beech, hemlock, hickory, maple, oak, pine, poplar, red cedar, walnut

Wild plants: azalea, buttercup, daisy, dogwood, fern, goldenrod, iris, laurel, magnolia, pennyroyal, trillium, violet

Woodchucks make their homes in Kentucky's forests.

PLACES TO VISIT

Big Bone Lick State Park, near Union
During the Ice Age, many animals came to this spot to lick the area's salt springs. The bones of these prehistoric creatures have been preserved and are on display in the park.

Kentucky History Center, Frankfort
This museum invites visitors to journey back through time—from Daniel Boone and the Wilderness Road, to the Civil War and civil rights.

Kentucky Horse Park, Lexington
Horse lovers will enjoy learning about horse breeding and training at this horse park. Located on the park's grounds are stables, exhibits, the International Museum of the Horse, and of course, lots of horses.

Kentucky Opry, Benton
For a taste of bluegrass, country, and gospel music, visit this musical theater. Performances at the Opry feature some of the finest talent in Kentucky.

Land Between the Lakes, near Paducah
Located between Kentucky Lake and Lake Barley, this 170,000-acre peninsula is a great place to go fishing, hiking, and camping.

Lexington Children's Museum, Lexington

With more than 100 hands-on exhibits and activities on topics ranging from astronomy to dinosaurs, this museum has something for everyone.

Newport Aquarium, Newport

Visiting the Newport Aquarium is like visiting the depths of the ocean. Visitors walk through 200 feet of clear, underwater tunnels that contain thousands of sea creatures.

Red River Gorge Geologic Area, Daniel Boone National Forest

This park offers some of the best rock climbing in the country. Visitors can also hike along the park's nature trails and canoe on the Red River.

Schmidt's Museum of Coca-Cola Memorabilia, Elizabethtown

Located in a Coca-Cola bottling plant, this museum is dedicated to one of the world's most popular beverages. Displays include advertising memorabilia and collectibles that reflect Coca-Cola's place in American culture.

Speed Art Museum, Louisville

Kentucky's oldest and largest art museum, the Speed Art Museum houses work produced by European and American artists over the last 6,000 years.

A stone arch in
Red River Gorge

ANNUAL EVENTS

Land Between the Lakes Eagle Weekend, western Kentucky—*February*

My Old Kentucky Home Festival of Quilts, Bardstown—*March*

Dogwood Trail Celebration, Paducah—*April*

Kentucky Derby Festival, Louisville—*April–May*

International Bar-B-Q Festival, Owensboro—*May*

Shaker Festival, South Union—*June*

Blackberry Festival, Carlisle—*July*

Kentucky State Fair, Louisville—*August*

Corn Island Storytelling Festival, Louisville—*September*

Festival of the Horse, Georgetown—*October*

Christmas Sing in the Cave, Mammoth Cave National Park—*December*

LEARN MORE ABOUT KENTUCKY

BOOKS

General

Barrett, Tracy. *Kentucky*. New York: Benchmark Books, 1999. For older readers.

Fradin, Dennis Brindell. *Kentucky*. Chicago: Children's Press, 1993.

Smith, Adam, and Katherine Snow Smith. *A Historical Album of Kentucky*. Brookfield, CT: Millbrook Press, 1995.

Special Interest

Bernards, Neal. *All Out! The Kentucky Wildcats Story*. North Mankato, MN: Smart Apple Media, 1999. This book covers the triumphs and defeats of one of Kentucky's most successful college basketball teams.

Gravelle, Karen. *Growing Up in a Holler in the Mountains: An Appalachian Childhood*. New York: Franklin Watts, 1997. Set in southeastern Kentucky, this book explores life in the Appalachian region of the state. The author focuses on everyday life for 10-year-old Joseph Ratliff and his family and includes sidebars on historical and cultural information about the region.

Schulman, Arlene. *Muhammad Ali*. Minneapolis, MN: Lerner Publications Company, 2001. This book follows the fascinating life of the first boxer to win the Heavyweight Championship three times.

Streissguth, Tom. *Daniel Boone.* Minneapolis, MN: Carolrhoda Books, Inc., 2001. This biography for young readers describes the life of the famous frontiersman who blazed the Wilderness Road and established the first white settlement in Kentucky.

Wells, Rosemary. *Mary on Horseback: Three Mountain Stories.* New York: Dial Books for Young Readers, 1998. In the 1920s, Mary Breckinridge became the first nurse to give medical care to families living in the Appalachian Mountains of Kentucky. The author tells the inspiring stories of three families who were helped by Mary Breckinridge.

Fiction

Lawlor, Laurie. *Adventure on the Wilderness Road, 1775.* New York: Minstrel Books, 1999. Based on the experiences of an actual pioneer family, this book tells the story of 11-year-old Elizabeth Poage, her parents, and her three siblings. As she travels on foot to reach Daniel Boone's settlement in Kentucky, Elizabeth soon discovers that life on the frontier can be rough and lonely—but also an exciting adventure.

Lyon, George Ella. *Borrowed Children.* Lexington, KY: University Press of Kentucky, 1999. Ever since her mother became ill, 12-year-old Amanda Perritt has had to take care of a house full of brothers and sisters in the rural mountains of Kentucky. Amanda gets the chance to leave her life behind when she spends Christmas with her grandparents in Memphis.

WEBSITES

Commonwealth of Kentucky Homepage
<http://www.kydirect.net/>
Kentucky's official website includes information about the state's government, economy, transportation, and education.

Kentucky Tourism
<http://www.kytourism.com>
Kentucky's official tourism website features general information about activities and attractions throughout the Bluegrass State and travel information about specific cities.

Kentucky Newspapers
<http://www.floridalink.com/links/kentucky.htm>
Check out the latest news in Kentucky with this website, which features links to 38 of the state's newspapers.

PRONUNCIATION GUIDE

Appalachian Plateau (ap-uh-LAY-chuhn pla-TOH)

Bering Strait (BEHR-ihng STRAYT)

Cherokee (CHER-uh-kee)

Iroquois (IHR-uh-kwoy)

Lexington (LEHK-sing-tuhn)

Louisville (LOO-ih-vihl)

New Orleans (NOO OR-lee-uhns)

Owensboro (OH-uhnz-buhr-uh)

Paducah (puh-DOO-kuh)

Shawnee (shaw-NEE)

GLOSSARY

civil rights: the right of all citizens—regardless of race, religion, or sex—to enjoy life, liberty, property, and equal protection under the law

colony: a territory ruled by a country some distance away

erosion: the wearing away of the earth's surface by the forces of water, wind, or ice

knob: a small, rounded hill or mountain

plateau: a large, relatively flat area that stands above the surrounding land

reclamation: the process of rebuilding land that has been mined and making it usable for plants, animals, or people

surface mining: a method of mining minerals that lie near the surface of the earth. Dirt, rock, and other materials are removed to uncover the mineral.

swamp: a wetland permanently soaked with water. Woody plants (trees and shrubs) are the main form of vegetation in a swamp.

wildcatter: in Kentucky, a miner who takes coal from the ground illegally, without getting permission to mine

INDEX

PHOTO ACKNOWLEDGMENTS

Cover photographs by © Kevin R. Morris/CORBIS (right) and © Jerry Cooke/CORBIS (left); PresentationMaps.com, pp. 1, 8, 9, 43; © Kevin R. Morris/CORBIS, pp. 2–3, 14, 44; © David Muench/CORBIS, pp. 3, 17, 75; © Hal Horwitz/CORBIS, pp. 4, 7 (inset), 17 (inset), 39 (inset), 51 (inset); © Ric Ergenbright/CORBIS, pp. 6, 50 (top); © 1992 Daniel E. Dempster, pp. 7, 15, 38, 41, 42, 46 (bottom), 50 (bottom), 58, 79; Maslowski Photo, p. 10; © Kent & Donna Dannen, pp. 11, 12; Kentucky Department of Travel Development, pp. 13, 16 (top); TVA photo by Ed Ray, p. 16 (bottom); Laura Westlund, pp. 18, 70 (bottom); Tennessee State Museum, from a painting by Carlyle Urello, p. 19; © 1992 Adam Jones, pp. 20, 39, 61; The Filson Club, pp. 21, 22, 23, 25, 28, 33, 35; Virginia State Library and Archives, p. 24; R.G. Potter Collection, Photographic Archives, University of Louisville, p. 26; © Bettmann/CORBIS, pp. 29, 37, 69 (top); Library of Congress, pp. 30, 69 (second from top); The Kentucky Library, Western Kentucky University, pp. 31, 36; Arthur Y. Ford Albums, Photographic Archives, University of Louisville, p. 32; Canfield & Shark Collection, Photographic Archives, University of Louisville, p. 34; Kentucky Department of Parks, pp. 43, 46 (top); © Mary Ann Lyons/*The Courier Journal*, Louisville, p. 45; Owensboro-Daviess County Tourist Commission, p. 48; © Toyota Motor Manufacturing, Kentucky, Inc., p. 49; Charles Bertram, p. 51; Thomas Spellman, Office of Special Investigations, Kentucky, N.R.E.P.C., pp. 53, 55, 56, 57; © Kay Shaw, pp. 54, 80; Kentucky Division of Forestry, p. 59; Jack Lindstrom, p. 60; Tim Seeley, pp. 63, 71 (top), 72; The Ring Magazine, p. 66 (top); Independent Picture Service, pp. 66 (second from top), 69 (bottom); Photographic Archives, Alice Lloyd College, p. 66 (second from bottom); Virginia State Library and Archives, p. 66 (bottom); Janice Smith, p. 67 (top); Duncan Hines, p. 67 (second from top); AP Photo/*Brainerd Daily Dispatch*, Steve Kohls, p. 67 (second from bottom); Minneapolis Public Library and Information Center, p. 67 (bottom); Loretta Lynn Enterprises, p. 68 (top); © Dave G. Houser/CORBIS, p. 68 (second from top); National Baseball Library, Cooperstown, N.Y., p. 68 (second from bottom); Kentucky Fried Chicken, p. 68 (bottom); Illinois State University, p. 69 (second from bottom); Jean Matheny, p. 70 (top); © Joe McDonald/CORBIS, p. 73.